Philip Ardagh's Shortcuts

A FAST
AND FUNNY
GUIDE TO

Mary, Queen of Scots

Philip Ardagh's Shortcuts

Philip Ardagh's Shortcuts

A FAST AND FUNNY GUIDE TO

Mary, Queen of Scots

Illustrated by Mike Phillips

MACMILLAN CHILDREN'S BOOKS

For Francesca and Isabelle Laidlaw,
with all that Scottish blood in your veins

First published 2000 by Macmillan Children's Books

This edition published 2013 by Macmillan Children's Books
a division of Macmillan Publishers Limited
20 New Wharf Road, London N1 9RR
Basingstoke and Oxford
Associated companies throughout the world
www.panmacmillan.com

ISBN 978-1-4472-4025-9

Text copyright © Philip Ardagh 2000
Illustrations copyright © Mike Phillips 2000

The right of Philip Ardagh and Mike Phillips to be identified as the
author and illustrator of this work has been asserted by them in
accordance with the Copyright, Designs and Patents Act 1988.

1 3 5 7 9 8 6 4 2

A CIP catalogue record for this book is available from the British Library.

Printed and bound by CPI Group (UK) Ltd, Croydon CR0 4YY

CONTENTS

The Author's Drastically Chopped About
FAMILY TREE OF MARY QUEEN OF SCOTS
with loads of people cut out, so it doesn't get too cluttered

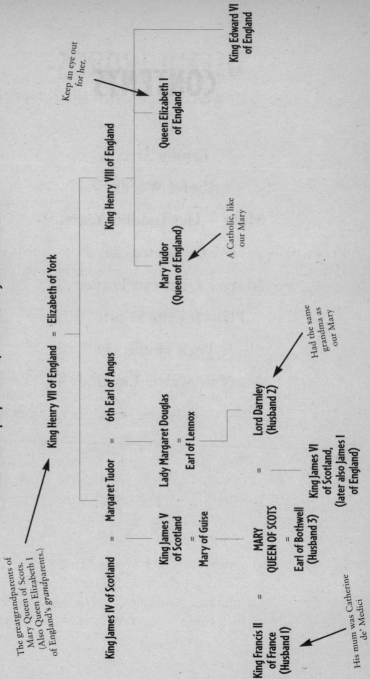

The greatgrandparents of Mary Queen of Scots. (Also Queen Elizabeth I of England's *grandparents*.)

King Henry VII of England = Elizabeth of York

Keep an eye out for her.

Queen Elizabeth I of England

King Edward VI of England

King Henry VIII of England

Mary Tudor (Queen of England)

A Catholic, like our Mary

Margaret Tudor = 6th Earl of Angus

King James IV of Scotland

Lady Margaret Douglas
=
Earl of Lennox

Lord Darnley (Husband 2)

Had the same grandma as our Mary

King James V of Scotland
=
Mary of Guise

King James VI of Scotland, (later also James I of England)

MARY QUEEN OF SCOTS
=
Earl of Bothwell (Husband 3)

King James II of France (Husband 1)

King Francis II of France (Husband 1)

His mum was Catherine de' Medici

USEFUL WORDS
(36.36% of which begin with the letter 'R')

Behead Either chopping someone's head off, if you're the one doing the beheading, or having your head chopped off, if you're the one being beheaded. Not too pleasant either way.

Calvinist A follower of the teachings of John Calvin, a Frenchman who was leader of the Protestant Reformation in France and Switzerland. Calvinists wore very simple clothes and wanted worship to be a serious no-frills business. Spoilsports.

Catholicism A branch of Christianity. Its leader, the pope, was (and still is) seen as God's Representative on Earth. Its full title is 'Roman Catholicism' and it's seen as 'High Church' with plenty of statues, incense and praying to saints.

Heir presumptive A person who expects to succeed a monarch (in the case of Mary, hoping to succeed Queen Elizabeth I of England) but may be ruled out by the birth of someone with a stronger claim to the throne (e.g. if Elizabeth marries and has a child).

Protestantism The branch of Christianity which is made up of all the Christians who aren't Roman Catholics. These include: Episcopalians, Quakers, Presbyterians, Puritans and Calvinists, and that's just a few. A real mixed bag.

Quadrangle A rectangular courtyard, usually with buildings on all four sides. Thrilling, huh?

Ratify To give formal approval to. Once treaties and agreements were signed, it was often still up to the monarch to ratify them – giving them the final 'OK'.

Regent Someone who rules on behalf of the monarch, usually if the monarch is too ill, too mad or too young (or sometimes all three).

Rosary A string of beads used by Catholics to count a special series of prayers which are also called 'the rosary'.

Rosery A garden full of roses. (Just thought I'd mention it.)

Scottish Reformation The 're-forming' of Scotland from a Catholic to a Protestant state.

MARY – THE TODDLER YEARS

Mary Queen of Scots wasn't born 'Mary Queen of Scots' but 'Mary Stuart'. She was the daughter of King James V of Scotland and his French wife, Mary of Guise. Mary – *our* Mary – was born on either the 7th or 8th of December 1542, at the palace of Linlithgow. No one seems to be sure which date it was but, with 8 December being the Feast of the Immaculate Conception of the Virgin Mary, Mary herself always called the 8th her birthday.

RUMOUR, RUMOUR EVERYWHERE

Mary had hardly been born before rumours started spreading about her. One was that she was terribly frail, another was that she was dead, and yet another rumour was that she was, in fact, a boy. It depended upon who you were as to which rumour you chose to believe! The Scots wanted to believe their royal baby was a boy, so that their king would have a son and heir. The English (under King Henry VIII) wanted to believe the child dead, so that James V of Scotland would have no one to succeed him. Another rumour was that the baby had been christened Elizabeth, the name of her cousin whom – if you stick around to find out – was to be the person behind her tragic downfall. (Sob! Wail!)

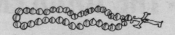

THE ENGLISH AND THE SCOTS

Today, England and Scotland are a part of what we call the United Kingdom, but back then they weren't. Although King Henry VIII of England was the uncle of Mary's dad, there was no love lost between them or between the English and the Scots. They were sworn enemies. Henry VIII of England had three children by three different wives: Mary Tudor (yup, another Mary, just to make things confusing), Elizabeth and Edward.

THE WORST OF TIMES

Mary – yes, *our* Mary, later Queen of Scots – was born just a few days after a battle between the Scottish and the English. The Battle of Solway Moss, as it became known, was a terrible defeat for her father's troops. Many Scotsmen died and, equally embarrassingly, over 1,000 Scottish noblemen were taken back to London as prisoners. King James V was horrified and heartbroken. He went to bed and never got up again, dying of shame on 14 December 1542. Both of Mary's baby brothers had died before she was born so, less than a week after her birth, Mary Stuart was now Queen Mary of Scotland or, to put it another way, really was Mary Queen of Scots.

WE CHARGE AT THE ENGLISH ON MY COUNT. ONE, TWO ...

TO RULE IN HER STEAD

With Mary Queen of Scots just a tiny baby, the most pressing matter was who should rule Scotland on her behalf? Her mother couldn't, of course. Things just weren't done that way. There were two separate claims as to how this job should be carried out. The Earl of Arran claimed that he should be sole regent until Mary was old enough to rule Scotland herself because, as head of the house of Hamilton, this was his hereditary right. The Hamilton Clan were another branch of the Scottish royal family. A cardinal called Beaton, however, claimed that Scotland shouldn't be ruled by one man but be overseen by a council of five governors (one of which would, indeed, be Arran), with the cardinal at its head! Cardinal Beaton claimed that this was what King James V had wanted and produced a will to prove it.

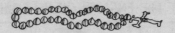

UNRELIABLE EARL & CRAFTY CARDINAL

The Earl of Arran was an important man and, if Mary Queen of Scots died, he had a perfectly good claim to the throne of Scotland in his own right. As choice for sole regent, though, he was far from ideal. He was notoriously indecisive and unreliable, if not a little unstable. Cardinal Beaton, the Archbishop of St Andrews, was unreliable in another way. This so-called will of the late King James V he'd produced was very probably a forgery.

VICTORY AND ARREST

Unreliable or not, the Earl of Arran won the day and became sole regent of Scotland, to rule on Mary's behalf until she 'came of age'. Cardinal Beaton, meanwhile, was arrested. The Scottish noblemen who'd been taken prisoner after the Battle of Solway Moss had been released by Henry VIII of England and returned to Scotland.

Whilst in England, many of these men had become sympathetic to Henry's Protestant, English cause, and didn't want to see a Catholic cardinal with so much influence in Scotland. The Earl of Arran himself had abandoned his Catholic faith.

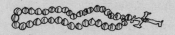

CHURCH OF ENGLAND, CHURCH OF ROME

Like most of Europe, England had been a Catholic country, answerable to the Catholic Church and His Holiness the Pope in Rome. Following, amongst other things, his difficulty in divorcing his first wife, Henry VIII of England had broken free of the pope and the Roman Catholic Church, putting himself at the head of his own church in his own country. The Scottish monarchy, meanwhile – if not all the Scots themselves – remained staunchly Catholic and Mary's mother and late father were no exception. With James V dead and Mary still a baby, much Scottish power now lay with pro-Protestant noblemen.

A MARRIAGE OF CONVENIENCE

King Henry VIII of England was now ready to push matters even further. He wanted to be absolutely sure of his power over the troublesome Scots just north of the border. The young – and, boy do I mean *young* – Mary Queen of Scots presented him with an ideal opportunity. What if Henry VIII's son Edward, heir to the English throne, was to marry Mary when they were both old enough? That way, their two countries could become united and, being the male, Edward would, in effect, become king of both countries too. Although Mary wasn't yet a year old, and Edward not yet six, the Treaties of Greenwich were drawn up on 1 July 1543, betrothing them to each other. Mary's mother and the Scottish court couldn't really say 'no'. They'd recently been defeated by Henry, remember.

THE TIDE TURNS

By the summer of 1543, Cardinal Beaton – whose first name was David, by the way, should anyone ask – was a free man, having somehow managed to escape from his imprisonment. He spent much of his time preaching pro-Catholic, pro-French ideas. Why pro-French? Because the French were Catholics, because Mary's mother was French and because the French were the worst enemies of Henry

14

VIII and the English. Two other influential pro-Catholic, pro-French Scotsmen were the Earl of Arran's own half-brother, the Abbot of Paisley, and the Earl of Lennox. All of them managed to influence the sole governor, Arran, that perhaps sucking up to the Protestant English wasn't such a good idea after all.

A PLACE OF SAFETY

The ink was barely dry on the Treaties of Greenwich when news reached Henry VIII in England that there were French ships just off the Scottish coast. Henry was worried that they were coming to try to snatch the baby Mary Queen of Scots. He sent word to Scotland that she must be moved from Linlithgow Palace to somewhere safer. The decision was, indeed, then made to move her . . . but to protect Mary from the English as much as the French! On 21 July 1543, Cardinal Beaton and 7,000 loyal Catholic followers marched from Stirling to Linlithgow, to insist that Mary come back with them and live in Stirling Castle.

A MIGHTY STRONGHOLD

High above the town of Stirling, Stirling Castle was thought to be one of the safest castles in Scotland, with a commanding view of any approaching enemies, and with impressive defences. Once safely inside, Henry VIII wanted baby Mary to be in the care of his own envoy, the Englishman Sir Ralph Sadler. After all, she would be married to his son one day, so didn't Henry have a right to demand such things? The Scots didn't think so. Mary's four guardians were to be the Scottish lords: Graham, Lindsay,

Livingston (without an 'e') and Erskine, all chosen by the pro-Arran Protestant Earl of Glencairn.

CORONATION STATIONS

History might have turned out very different if Henry VIII of England hadn't finally gone too far. At one stage he tried to bribe Cardinal Beaton to give up his life in the Catholic Church and to throw in his lot with the English. Then the English impounded a Scottish merchant ship due to trade with the English's dreaded enemies, the French . . . and the Earl of Arran finally decided that enough was enough. On 8 September 1543, the regent attended a Catholic mass and switched his support to Cardinal Beaton and the pro-French. The following day, the nine-month-old Mary was crowned queen.

THE FRENCH CONNECTION

Now that the Scots were allies of the French and now that the dauphin, Prince Henri, and Catherine de' Medici of France had had a little baby boy – Francis, in January 1544

– the idea that Mary should marry the English heir Edward seemed crazy. Surely it made much more sense for the Catholic, half-French Mary Queen of Scots to be engaged to the dauphin's Catholic, French son? It was simple speculation at this stage, but it soon reached Henry VIII's ears and he didn't like what he heard.

ENGLAND'S REVENGE

Henry VIII could see that all his Scottish scheming was getting him exactly nowhere. His plans were falling apart around him, so he needed to act. He decided his best approach was to make the Scottish realize just how ruthless and powerful the English were. He would try to woo them (win them over) with a show of strength, not promises. The terror which followed therefore became known as the 'rough wooing'. Homes, villages, farmland and gardens were laid waste. Even the city of Edinburgh was burnt and the abbey and Holyrood Palace ransacked. The English later captured merchant ships and even vandalized the tombs of ancient Scottish heroes.

ENEMIES WITHIN

The English weren't the only cause of unrest in Scotland, however. There were those Scots who were unhappy with the power and wealth of the Catholic Church in their country. In March 1546, for example, a Protestant preacher named George Wishart was burnt at St Andrews Castle watched by, amongst others, Cardinal Beaton and his bishops. Three months later, it was the cardinal's turn to come to a sticky end. Disguised as masons sent to repair the castle, a group of Scottish Lords from Fife stabbed the cardinal, took over the castle and hung his naked and horribly mutilated body from one of its towers for all to see. Later, the body was taken down and pickled in a barrel of salt - yes, that's what I said: *pickled in a barrel of salt* - and kept in the 'Bottle Dungeon' for a year or so! The Earl of Arran's forces laid siege to the castle which held out against them for an impressive fourteen months. It came to an end on 30 July 1547 when French forces intervened. Many of those defenders who weren't executed were taken as prisoners to France.

THE BATTLE OF PINKIE CLEUGH

1547 was also the year that saw England's most serious assault on Mary's Scotland so far. The Scots knew that an attack was coming and about 36,000 people, from all four corners of the country – if Scotland has corners – headed for Edinburgh. The battle actually took place at Pinkie Cleugh, near the town of Musselburgh. The Scottish forces were up on a ridge, under the command of the Earl of Arran himself. It was a strong, defensive position, so your guess is as good as mine why the earl chose to *attack* instead! The English troops were far better trained and slaughtered the Scots.

MAKE INCHMAHONE MY HOME!

With the English commander, Somerset, on the loose in the Scottish lowlands, it was decided that Stirling Castle was no longer the safest place for Mary Queen of Scots to be. Still under five years old, the queen was moved to a priory on Inchmahone, which was a tiny island in a lake not far from Stirling. She was only there for about three weeks but, because it was such a fairytale setting, many myths have grown up about her time there. In fact, she was soon back at Stirling and, in February 1548, was moved to Dumbarton Castle on the west coast.

TO THE RESCUE!

By July 1548, Prince Henri, the dauphin, had become King Henri II of France and Catherine de' Medici his queen. Their son Francis was now dauphin and it was agreed that Mary Queen of Scots should become engaged to *him* instead of the English prince. The French also agreed to defend Scotland against the English if needs be.

If Mary was to marry the new dauphin, then it was agreed that she must be brought up in the French court. In July, one of King Henri II of France's own ships arrived, with escorts, at Dumbarton on the west coast. Sadly, Mary's own mother, Mary of Guise, was to remain in Scotland. It would be the responsibility of the French king and queen to bring up little Mary. Life could be very tough like that, when it came to arranged marriages. So, on 7 August 1548, Mary said a sad farewell to her mum, and climbed aboard the ship, ready to set sail for France and a new chapter in her life . . .

EN FRANCE
(AS THE FRENCH SAY)

Although Mary's mum was French, Mary could only speak Scots when she arrived in France, which is fair enough if you're five and Scottish. After a stormy crossing – during which it was reported that she was the only one who wasn't seasick – Mary took to France like a duck to water. This is hardly surprising, because King Henri and Queen Catherine made her so welcome. Later, the king described her as being 'the most perfect child I have ever seen'.

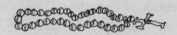

THE FOUR MARIES

Amongst plenty of other things, Mary Queen of Scots is famous for being accompanied to France by the 'Four Maries'. All of noble birth, they were: Mary Beaton, Mary Fleming, Mary Livingston (without an 'e') and Mary Seton . . . as if there weren't enough people called Mary in this book already! Before you ask: yes, Mary Beaton was a relative of Cardinal Beaton, but she was from a different branch of the family; and, yes, Mary Livingston (without an 'e') was related to the Lord Livingston (without an 'e') named in the bogus will of James V as one of the proposed five governors of Scotland, who had since - by the way - become one of Mary's guardians. Mary Fleming was of 'royal Scottish blood' and Mary Seton's mother, a Frenchwoman, had first come to Scotland as a lady-in-waiting to Mary's own mother. It was a small world!

IN COURT AT LAST

After two months in France, Mary finally arrived at the French royal court on 9 October 1548. King Henri and his wife Catherine de' Medici had seven children altogether. After Francis (the dauphin) came Elisabeth – no, not that one, you're thinking of Henry VIII of England's daughter – Claude (a girl), Charles, Henry, another Francis and, last but not least, Marguerite. None of them was in the best of health.

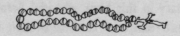

NOT TRUE! NOT TRUE!

No book about Mary Queen of Scots would be complete without the marmalade myth, even though it's not true. The story goes that the ever-popular young Mary was ill in bed and, down in the palace kitchens a sad chef was stirring a bowl of oranges, muttering 'Marie est malade', which is French for 'Mary is ill', over and over again as he stirred. Suddenly he noticed that the oranges had became what we now think of as marmalade. He had invented a new treat, which he named especially after the occasion! The truth be told, the word 'marmalade' comes from the Portuguese word for a fruit called a quince – not from 'Marie est malade' – and marmalade had been around for years by then anyway!

FRIENDSHIPS ARE FORMED

With the Four Maries sent to be educated at the convent of Poissy by nuns, Mary had to make new friends. Her best friend was Princess Elisabeth. She didn't actually meet Elisabeth's father, the king, until November and he was instantly charmed by her. As she quickly learnt French, the two would sometimes talk for hours. The next ten years or so were the most carefree in her life.

A VISIT FROM HER MOTHER

In September 1550, Mary's mother, Mary of Guise, came to the French court to see her. Mary was overjoyed! This would be the first time they'd met in over two years. Mother and daughter were delighted to be reunited and Mary of Guise was made very welcome by King Henri and Queen Catherine. Mary's mum stayed for a year before heading back to Scotland, via London.

MARRIAGE AT LAST

Unlike the proposed marriage between Mary Queen of Scots and Prince Edward of England, the marriage between Mary Queen of Scots and the dauphin, Francis, did take place. On Sunday 24 April 1558 Mary (aged fifteen) and Francis (aged fourteen) were married in the famous cathedral of Notre Dame, following their official engagement on 19 April. This had resulted from plenty of behind-the-scenes wheeler-dealing between French officials and Scottish envoys, led by Mary's granny, Antoinette of Guise. Antoinette was acting on behalf of Mary's mum, who'd become Scotland's regent, governing the country until Mary was old enough.

THE TWO TREATIES

Before Mary and Francis were married, Scottish envoys signed a treaty with the French agreeing what would happen if one or the other died. It was all fair and square. But what they didn't know about was the *second* treaty. These secret papers contained far more explosive agreements between Mary Queen of Scots and the French

. . . and, when you read what she agreed to, you'll see why it was so hush hush. First off, it was agreed that if Mary died without children, Scotland would automatically be governed by France (becoming little more than a French province). Secondly, Scotland, its treasury and income would be handed over to France until every penny that France had spent on defending it had been repaid (which the French could make sure was never). And, finally, whatever agreements Mary might enter into later that went against what was agreed here would be null and void . . . which was very far-sighted and sneaky of them. It may seem amazing that Mary agreed to sign these arrangements, but it's worth remembering that she was still just a girl and loved and trusted those around her.

DEATH OF 'THE OTHER' MARY

In November 1558, events in England became very important to Mary Queen of Scots. The English monarch, Queen Mary [Tudor], Henry VIII's Roman Catholic daughter, died. King Henri II of France now declared his daughter-in-law, *our* Mary, to be Queen of England as well as Scotland. He insisted she use the English royal coat-of-arms as her own. The English, meanwhile, crowned Mary Tudor's half-sister 'Queen Elizabeth I of England'.

THE STUART CLAIM

So what made the French king think Mary Queen of Scots had a right to the English throne? Let me try to explain. Here goes: Mary Tudor's dad and mum were Henry VIII and Catherine of Aragon. Henry then divorced Catherine and married Anne Boleyn. They had a daughter, Elizabeth. In the eyes of the Catholic Church, however, there was no such thing as divorce, so Henry was still married to Aragon which meant that Elizabeth was illegitimate – born outside marriage – so couldn't inherit the English throne. Who did that leave? Well, Mary Queen of Scots's greatgrandfather was Elizabeth's grandfather, King Henry VII of England so, the French argued, Mary was the only legitimate, living descendant of that king and should, therefore, be crowned Queen of England. Simple . . . I *don't* think.

ANOTHER DEATH, ANOTHER CROWN

Soon another death led to far more immediate changes for our Mary. In June 1559, King Henri II of France was enjoying a good day's jousting. To round off the day, he challenged Jacques de Lorge, the Count of Montgomery, to one last joust. According to some versions of events, Queen Catherine de' Medici pleaded with her husband not to, having had two premonitions that this would end in disaster. Montgomery is supposed to have refused to fight, until his king ordered him to . . . As it was, Montgomery's lance shattered, one huge splinter piercing the king's eye and the other his throat. He died on 10 July. Mary's husband was no longer dauphin but King of France. She was now its sixteen-year-old queen.

MARY – QUEEN OF FRANCE

Sadly, this is one of the shortest chapters in any *Shortcuts* biography so far. The reason is simple. Mary Queen of Scots wasn't to be Mary Queen of France for very long.

A BAD YEAR

The year 1560 was a terrible one for Mary. In June, her mum, Mary of Guise, died back in Scotland. When Mary heard the news she was heartbroken. Meanwhile, matters with England were still high on the agenda and, in July, it was agreed in the Treaty of Edinburgh that English troops would leave Scotland, so long as French troops did the same – with a few agreed exceptions – and that Mary and Francis would give up any claim to the English throne and recognize Elizabeth I as England's rightful queen. At the same time, both England and France would promise to stay out of Scottish affairs. The English troops did withdraw, but matters were then messed up when the Scottish Reformation burst onto the scene. Suddenly, Scotland was a Protestant country with a Catholic queen away in France. With Elizabeth being a Protestant queen, the Scots would be more likely to turn to *her* for help when needed than their own 'true' queen on the continent.

NOT THE HEALTHIEST OF CHAPS

Then there were the worries about Francis. The king had never been the healthiest of people (neither had Mary). He fainted on more than one occasion and his face was covered with worrying-looking blotches. Wild rumours spread around France that he had leprosy. Even worse, stories were told that he often washed in children's blood to try to cure himself! This was totally untrue, of course, but enough to make some people hide their kids when the young king was around! Crowned King Francis II on 18 September 1559, Mary's young husband died on 5 December 1560. Mary was Queen of France no longer. End of chapter.

PLANS FOR THE FUTURE

It is traditional for those in mourning for the dead to wear black. Although Mary shut herself away in a black room, talking to as few people as possible, she chose to wear *white* for the forty days of official mourning. There was little reason for her to remain in France after that, though. Francis's brother, Charles, was now King Charles IX, with her mother-in-law Catherine de' Medici acting as unofficial regent, governing the country on his behalf. What role was there for Mary?

MARRIAGE WITH SPAIN?

Mary's attentions were now turned to Spain, however. She was considering the possibility of marrying Don Carlos, heir to the Spanish throne with its mighty empire. Spain was a great power, and like Mary, Don Carlos was a Catholic. Not only that, the weather in Spain was much warmer and more pleasant than in Scotland, which she might otherwise return to. The downside was that, although the Spanish heir was sixteen, he weighed only five and a half stone and – after falling down stairs when chasing after a chambermaid – he often had fits of homicidal mania. (In other words, he'd try to kill people.) If that wasn't sad and bad enough, he'd fallen head-over-heels in love with his own stepmother! Not the ideal choice for Husband Number Two, perhaps?

ENGLAND SUCKS UP

The English court was eager to have Mary on their side and the Earl of Bedford was sent to France in February 1561, to offer Queen Elizabeth's condolences at the death of her husband. A young Englishman named Lord Darnley also paid a visit, at his mother's request.

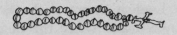

DASHING DARNLEY

Lord Darnley was, in fact, a title. His family name was Henry Stuart and he and Mary Queen of Scots shared the same grandmother, Margaret Tudor, which made them cousins. (Whereas Mary's grandfather had been Margaret's first husband, King James IV of Scotland, *his* grandfather had been her second husband, the 6th Earl of Angus.) He had royal Scottish AND English blood in him. Darnley had first met Mary at her husband Francis's coronation. His mother had sent Darnley back to France in the hope that her dashing son might be considered a good prospect as a second husband for Mary. But Mary wasn't interested in Lord Darnley yet. [Y-E-T.]

HER MIND IS MADE UP

Mary could have stayed in France as a dowager queen – widow of a dead monarch – for the rest of her days. But, for whatever reason, she decided to return 'home' to the country she hadn't set foot in since she was a tiny tot. But first Mary wanted Queen Elizabeth I of England to guarantee her 'safe passage'. Mary sent an envoy named d'Oysel to the English court with the request, which Elizabeth blankly refused. When the English ambassador, Sir Nigel Throckmorton, heard the news, he was puzzled. Surely it would be better for England for Mary to be nearer to home and out of the way up in Scotland, rather than in the thick of things on the continent?

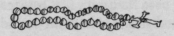

THE UNRESOLVED TREATY

Another sticking point between Elizabeth Queen of England and Mary Queen of Scots went all the way back to the Treaty of Edinburgh in July 1560 (and all the way back to page 28). As you may remember, all was going fine until the Scottish Reformation meant that not everything agreed in the treaty was put into action. As a result, Mary had never bothered to ratify the treaty for the Scots. Ratify means 'give the final OK to', so, without Mary's ratification, the treaty was never officially and finally agreed. It had been one of Throckmorton's many jobs to persuade Mary to ratify it now.

ALL ABOARD!

Mary now took a more informal approach, writing Queen Elizabeth a personal letter, in the friendliest of terms, asking for safe passage . . . but didn't wait for a reply before acting. She said her 'goodbyes' then prepared to leave. As well as three of her uncles, Mary travelled back to Scotland with the 'Four Maries' she'd first come over with: Seton, Beaton, Livingston and Fleming.

It had been suggested to our Mary that she leave her jewellery behind for safety's sake. She was quick to point out that, if the ship was safe enough for her, it was safe enough for her jewels! Now, she was heading home . . .

BACK HOME

Mary's ships did indeed run into English ships on the voyage home, but only to send her greetings. Queen Elizabeth I of England had responded to Mary's latest letter in a friendly manner. On Tuesday 19 August 1561, Mary set foot on Scottish soil for the first time in thirteen years, after landing at the port of Leith. It was nine o'clock in the morning, the place was thick with mist and no one had expected her to arrive so soon. There were no large crowds to greet her and no lodging had been arranged for her. She had lunch and a quick nap at the home of one Andrew Lamb.

TO HOLYROOD!

After this, Mary Queen of Scots was escorted to Holyrood Palace, just outside the walls of the city of Edinburgh. She was flanked by a number of Scottish lords, including the Protestant Earl of Argyll and a man named James Stewart who was, in fact, her half-brother.

Even though Scotland was now pretty much ruled by the Protestant Church, guided by the Protestant reformer John Knox – ignore the 'K', it was pronounced 'nox' – and though Mary herself was Catholic, there was a fair bit of rejoicing at their queen's arrival. Bonfires were lit to celebrate her return.

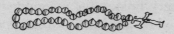

A RESTLESS NIGHT

Mary's first night back in Scotland, in her suite of rooms at Holyrood, is famous for its awfulness. Five or six hundred well-wishers gathered outside the palace and began playing and singing psalms to welcome Mary Queen of Scots home. The singing was, apparently, tuneless and the playing dreadful too. Legend has it that it was the sound of the bagpipes that kept Mary awake but, in fact, the crowd played fiddles and another type of stringed instrument called a rebec. The next morning, Queen Mary diplomatically pronounced that the experience had been a delight!

Mary thought that she was being equally diplomatic when it came to practising her religion. She would stick to her Catholic beliefs but perform the rights – attend mass and so on – in private. Despite this, when news leaked out that their queen was to attend her first mass in the 'chapel royal' in the palace, angry Protestant reformers tried to burst in, but were prevented by her half-brother! Mary was quick to act. She made it clear that no one (including her) would interfere with the new state religion of Protestantism, on the pain of death, but, at the same time, no one must interfere with the beliefs of those Catholics who'd come back from France . . . also on the pain of death. John Knox was far from thrilled.

JOHN KNOX

John Knox had started life as a Catholic but ended up supporting the murderers of Cardinal Beaton in St Andrew's Castle and was taken prisoner. Later, he went to Protestant England but, when Catholic Mary Tudor became queen, he'd nipped over to the continent, where he became a Calvinist. Returning to Scotland, he converted many people to Protestantism, preached violence and openly hated Mary.

BUILDING BRIDGES

Neither 'side' did the other any favours, and Mary spent many of her first months in Scotland trying to find a fair balance for both Protestants and Catholics. At the same time, she was eager to build a friendship with her cousin, Queen Elizabeth, over in England. Less than two weeks after her return home, Mary sent William Maitland to the English court as her envoy. The main aim was simple: if Mary ratified the treaty of Edinburgh for Elizabeth (that business on page 32), Elizabeth should officially recognize Mary as next in line to the English throne if she, Elizabeth, had no children to succeed her. Although Queen Elizabeth was quick to stress that she'd far rather Mary succeed her than some of the other possibilities, she wouldn't commit herself to declaring a choice publicly. She claimed that if she agreed to this, Mary would probably end up the centre of attention for plots to overthrow her and to put Mary on the throne of England.

MR & MRS QUEEN

Although both wanted something from the other – Elizabeth wanted Mary to ratify a slightly revised Treaty of Edinburgh and Mary wanted to be recognized as 'heir presumptive' – they wrote a series of friendly letters to each other, for a while. Mary is said to have said as a joke that it was a pity that neither she nor Elizabeth was a man because, if one them had been, then they could have got married and unified the thrones of England and Scotland. This had already occurred to Throckmorton!

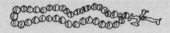

SCOTS PLOTS

At this time, all was not peace and quiet in Scotland either. There were many plots between groups of Protestant Scottish nobles trying to discredit Catholic Scottish nobles, and vice versa. The 3rd Earl of Arran sent a coded message stating that the Earl of Bothwell had tried to get him involved in a plot to kidnap Mary and rule Scotland in her place! Arran's own family thought him quite mad, and had already locked him up in the family castle. Despite this, Mary had Bothwell locked up in Edinburgh Castle, just in case. Arran managed to escape from his prison in real comic-book style. He really did climb out of the window on a rope made out of sheets knotted together!

GHASTLY GORDON

In August 1562, Mary paid her first visit to the highlands of her kingdom. Here, she ran into a spot of bother with Sir John Gordon, one of the twelve children of the 4th Earl of Huntly. Gordon planned to abduct the queen for real, and followed the royal party. Rumour spread that 1,000 horsemen from the Gordon clan were waiting to pounce but, if they were, they never put in an appearance. Huntly and Gordon were soon declared outlaws. The Earl promptly died of a heart attack when faced by troops loyal to Queen Mary. His dead body was then embalmed and brought to the Scottish Parliament to be tried for treason. His corpse was found guilty and beheaded!!! It was a living Sir John Gordon who was executed in the queen's presence. The executioner did such a botched job that Mary broke down and wept.

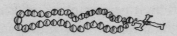

ANOTHER NUTTER?

Amongst the party who'd come from France to Scotland with Mary Queen of Scots was the Frenchman Pierre de Châtelard. He soon declared an undying passion for the queen, and she seemed to like his harmless flirting . . . until he was caught hiding under her bed and she had him kicked out of court. The following night he burst in on her, and Mary called for her half-brother (now the Earl of Moray) to stab him. Instead, Châtelard was publicly tried and executed. Had he been a madman, genuinely believing he was in love with the queen? Or had he been out to ruin her reputation? No one knows.

HUNT FOR A HUBBY

Mary hadn't given up hope in the hunt for a husband and let everyone know that she still hadn't ruled out the possibility of marrying Don Carlos of Spain. John Knox was horrified at the thought of her marrying another *Catholic*. Queen Elizabeth I of England was horrified too, and was swift to act. Knowing that her cousin Mary was keen to be named 'heir presumptive' of England, Elizabeth thought she might have enough influence over her to be able to get involved in a little matchmaking. Having sworn that she'd never marry anyone herself, Elizabeth suggested her own favourite, Lord Robert Dudley, as a husband to Mary.

DASHING DARNLEY RETURNS

Then, in February 1565, Mary's cousin, dashing Lord Darnley, suddenly paid a visit to Scotland. Whether it was Elizabeth or some of her advisors who were trying to push forward Darnley is uncertain . . . but it had the desired effect. Mary really took a liking to him after he fell ill at Stirling Castle. She spent more and more time at his bedside and fell head-over-heels in love with him. All thoughts of carefully arranged, politically clever marriages were forgotten. She would marry Darnley whatever the cost.

DARNLEY TURNS DASTARDLY

And marry they did, in July 1565, despite the fact that it nearly led to civil war in Scotland. Darnley was another Catholic, and she even gave him the title 'King of Scotland'. The Protestants were outraged. Suddenly, Mary's own half-brother would have nothing to do with her. Darnley, meanwhile, revealed his nastier side. He was a cruel, drunken swine. Upset and pregnant, Mary turned to her secretary, David Riccio – sometimes spelled Rizzio – for comfort. Egged on by certain Scottish lords (and convinced that Mary was being more than just comforted by Riccio), Darnley arranged for the secretary's murder.

EXIT RICCIO

On 9 March 1566, Mary was having supper with Riccio and a group of friends in her suite in Holyrood Palace.

Suddenly, Darnley burst in from his private staircase, followed closely by Lord Ruthven. Darnley stood in front of his pregnant wife, preventing her from helping her poor secretary, whilst Ruthven stabbed Riccio over fifty – yes FIFTY – times. (Some say as many as sixty.) Though shocked and horrified, with the dying Riccio clutching the hem of her dress, Mary was herself unhurt. She gave birth to a healthy baby, James, three months later. Darnley claimed he'd been shielding his wife from Ruthven to protect her. Mary wasn't so sure.

AMBITIOUS BOTHWELL

Not surprisingly, Mary now hated Darnley, but what could she do? She turned to the Earl of Bothwell for help. After weeping at Riccio's murder, Mary said, 'No more tears now; I will think upon revenge'. And revenge was what she would have. The Earl of Bothwell was the same Bothwell who'd been thrown into Edinburgh Castle without trial back on page 38. By now he was back in the queen's favour.

UNDER THE WEATHER

With her son and heir, James, safely tucked away at Stirling Castle, under the care of the Earl of Mar and the Erskine family, Mary made it clear that it was James who would succeed her, not her husband Darnley. Mary was ill and, in an age when people were far more likely to die from an illness, she was obviously concerned to make this matter v-e-r-y c-l-e-a-r. Throughout her illness, Darnley didn't even bother to pretend to be a devoted husband, so didn't even visit her once.

THE DEATH OF DIABOLICAL DARNLEY

The following January, 1567, Darnley fell ill in Glasgow and Mary was kind enough to send her doctor to him – they were no longer living together. She later set out to bring him back to Edinburgh to get better. He chose to stay in a house just on the edge of the city in a quadrangle known as the Kirk-o'-Field.

On 10 February 1567, at about two o'clock in the morning, there was a huge explosion at the house. Darnley's body either went flying out of the bed, up in the air and landed some distance away with what would have been a very nasty squelch . . . or it was placed there to look like that had happened (and the explosion had been designed to cover up the real murder) . . . or he'd heard the explosives being planted, had tried to escape and had been caught. Either way, it wasn't the explosion that killed him.

MARY IN MOURNING . . . AGAIN

Mary Queen of Scots went into mourning once more, this time wearing the more traditional black. Many people have argued that she was either behind the plot to kill Darnley, or knew about it, because it was public knowledge that the explosion was arranged by Bothwell and a group of Scottish lords. But just how involved was the queen? Nowadays, many historians argue that Mary probably didn't know what Bothwell was up to. In March, a private prosecution of Bothwell was brought before parliament, but he was found 'not guilty' and acquitted.

BAD TO WORSE

On 21 April 1567, Mary visited her baby, James, at Stirling Castle. She played with him the whole of the next day too, blissfully unaware that this would be the very last time that they would be together. She would never see her son again. On the 23rd, Mary headed for home. Unwell, she was travelling with a party of just over 300 people, which was considered a small number for a royal party. On 24 April, about six miles from Edinburgh, Bothwell appeared with a private army of 800 men . . .

A KIDNAP BY ANY OTHER NAME

Although Bothwell claimed that there was 'danger' in Edinburgh and that he'd come to take Mary to Dunbar Castle where she'd be out of harm's way, it was clear what he was up to. He planned to kidnap his queen, and many of Mary's party realized this and were prepared to fight. Heavily outnumbered, eager to avoid bloodshed and resigned to her fate, Mary agreed to go with Bothwell. Back in Edinburgh, the alarm was raised and a rescue was planned. But it was too late to thwart Boswell's scheme. By amazing coincidence Mary's kidnap took place on the ninth anniversary of her marriage to her first husband, Francis.

HUSBAND NUMBER THREE

Amazingly, on 15 May 1567, Bothwell now married Mary at Holyrood! Did he force her or had she fallen in love with him? Who knows . . . the outcome was still the same. The Scots were horrified. Mary's previous husband had only been dead for three months and, more likely than not, he'd been murdered by the man she was now married to! And Bothwell had had to divorce his own sick wife to marry Mary. The Protestant lords now united against them.

DEFEAT!

On Sunday 15 June, the rebel army marched out of Edinburgh. They met Bothwell's 'royal' troops at Carberry Hill. Mary was eventually captured and taken back to Edinburgh. Along the way, she was showered with insults. The most common cry seems to have been 'Murderess!'. After Edinburgh, she became a prisoner in a castle on an island in the middle of Lochleven and forced to abdicate – to give up the throne. Bothwell, meanwhile, fled the country. On 29 July 1567, Mary's son – just over a year old – was crowned King James VI of Scotland. To some, our Mary was no longer seen as 'Queen of Scots'.

WILY WILLY!

Even though Mary was stuck on an island in a middle of a loch miles from Edinburgh, she wasn't without friends. After ten months imprisonment, a group of them helped her to escape. In the castle there were members of the Douglas family, including one young Willy Douglas. A May Day pageant at the castle was arranged for 2 May 1568 and there were plenty of strangers about. Willy stole a set of keys to the main gates and had Mary boldly walk right through them, in disguise. She was then bundled into a boat and rowed to freedom. Willy Douglas remained in Mary's service right up until she died.

A FINAL STAND

Mary still had her supporters *outside* the castle too. She'd soon gathered together an army of 5,000 loyal Scots and went to face her half-brother (the Earl of Moray)'s army of about 3,000 at the village of Langside. Mary's troops were under the command of the Earl of Argyll and, unfortunately, he either fainted or deliberately betrayed the queen. (After all, the Earl of Moray was his brother-in-law!) The result was a defeat for Mary. She fled.

WE'RE READY TO ATTACK THE ENEMIES OF THE QUEEN, YOUR LORDSHIP

ER... RIGHT. DO I HAVE TIME TO NIP HOME AND CHANGE MY SHIRT? THIS ONE'S A BIT GRUBBY!

DECISIONS, DECISIONS

Now Mary had to make one of the momentous decisions of her life. She didn't feel she could stay in Scotland any longer, but where should she go? The obvious answer was France. It was a Catholic country where she'd once been queen and they were bound to support her against the Protestants. Instead, Mary decided to seek sanctuary in England. It was a Protestant country ruled by a queen she'd never met and with whom she'd often disagreed. But Mary's mind was made up. Perhaps she held out the hope that she might one day rule England after all.

A FINAL FAREWELL

On Sunday 16 May 1568, Mary stepped into a fishing boat and, at three o'clock, left the shores of Scotland for the very last time. The journey across the Solway Firth was only four hours and England loomed ever-larger up ahead of her. With her were about twenty loyal followers and servants. There was no turning back.

MARY IN MERRIE ENGLAND

Once in England – Mary landed in Cumberland (not to be muddled with *Cu*cumberland, home of the long green vegetable) – she immediately wrote to her cousin, Queen Elizabeth, for help. Finding herself held a semi-prisoner in Carlisle Castle, Mary awaited news from the English court. Not surprisingly, the Protestant Queen Elizabeth had no intention of helping the Catholic Mary reclaim the throne of Scotland by force. And, anyway, wasn't it quite useful having her locked up where she couldn't do any mischief?

DARN IT, DARNLEY!

Then there was the small matter of whether Mary had played a part in the murder of Lord Darnley and the fact that she'd ended up marrying Bothwell, the number one suspect!!! Queen Elizabeth declared that Mary must allow her to judge her innocence or guilt before deciding to welcome her with open arms. Mary was furious.

THE CASE FOR THE DEFENCE

Mary was moved to Bolton Castle in Yorkshire. This, Elizabeth claimed, was so that Mary would be that bit nearer the English court . . . but it was still a good way off! Then the Conference of York began in October 1568. During the conference, an English panel, under the Duke of Norfolk, examined the evidence for and against Mary in the case of Darnley's murder. The case against Mary was brought by her own half-brother, the Earl of Moray, who was now regent to her son, King James VI. She was represented by a number of commissioners.

THE CASKET LETTERS

The Protestant Scots had produced a casket which, according to them, was jam-packed full of letters from Mary to Bothwell, supposedly 'proving' that she and Bothwell had been in love from the start and had plotted to kill Darnley together. These were presented to the panel at the conference and threw everyone into such turmoil that Queen Elizabeth ordered a new conference to be set up in Westminster. Today, the general opinion amongst most historians is that the 'casket letters' were in fact forgeries/ fakes/made-up/whopping great lies.

THE VERDICT

The panel's verdict when it came was very wishy-washy to say the least. In the end, Queen Elizabeth declared that there was no real proof that Mary herself was up to no good when it came to the death of Darnley. The result? Moray returned to Scotland . . . and Mary remained a prisoner in everything but name.

BESS OF HARDWICKE

Mary was moved yet *again*, this time to Tutbury Castle in Derbyshire, on the Staffordshire border. Mary'd made it clear that she'd rather be left 'bound hand and foot' in Bolton than be moved . . . but moved she was. Mary was now the responsibility of the Earl of Shrewsbury and his wife, 'Bess of Hardwicke'. In icy-cold Tutbury, Mary became ill. She moved to Bess's house, Chatsworth, and Mary took up a new hobby: embroidery. Mary sent gifts of embroidery left, right and centre, including to Queen Elizabeth. Examples still survive today.

FUMING ALL ROUND

At the same time, Mary was trying to divorce Bothwell and was showing more than a little interest in the 4th Duke of Norfolk . . . which was odd, because she'd never met him! He was not only the *only* duke in England at the time — weird but true — he was also very wealthy. Elizabeth blew her top, imagining that it was a plot for Mary to strengthen her power and respectability in England. Norfolk was thrown into the Tower of London, and Mary was sent straight back to Carlisle Castle, to a smaller suite of rooms, and was forbidden to send or receive letters.

UPRISING!

One of the reasons why Elizabeth had wanted Mary moved away from Yorkshire was because it was up north . . . and up north was where most of the unhappy English Catholics were! In November, some of them rebelled. The whole thing was badly organized and had little if anything to do with supporting Catholic Mary. The result? Mary was moved even *further* south, to Coventry Castle!

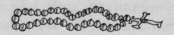

TROUBLE AT HOME

Things weren't all sweetness and light back in Scotland, either. Mary's half-brother, the Earl of Moray, was shot dead in Linlithgow

on 11 June 1570. A popular tale was that he was killed by a man whose wife had caught her death of cold when Moray forced her out into the snow. The truth be told, he was assassinated by one of the Hamilton clan. The new regent was the dead Darnley's father, the 4th Earl of Lennox. Back in England, Queen Elizabeth had had a fair amount of influence in his selection.

IT'S PLOT TIME!

There then followed a series of plots involving Mary . . . whether she liked it or not. The less ambitious ones were intended to help her escape. The more ambitious ones planned to put her on the throne of England! An early plot, including a Sir Thomas Gerard, was to somehow smuggle Mary out of Chatsworth and spirit her away to the Isle of Man. There were, however, far more famous plots . . .

THE RIDOLFI PLOT

Roberto Ridolfi was an Italian banker living in England. In 1570/71, he plotted for the Spanish to invade England via Holland. The hope was that the Catholics in England would then rise up and join the Spanish invaders and, together, they'd put Mary on the English throne. King Philip II of Spain was far from convinced about the Catholics-in-England-rising-up-and-joining-the-invaders part and said that, if Ridolfi was so sure that the English Catholics were ready to rise up against Elizabeth, he'd wait until that happened and *then* send the troops in. Not that any of this mattered because the plot was soon uncovered by Elizabeth's 'secret service'. One unfortunate plotter, the Duke of Norfolk (him again), was executed for his part in it. What couldn't be proved was whether Mary herself had been involved in the plot.

THE THROCKMORTON PLOT

Like the Ridolfi plot, the Throckmorton plot got its name from one of the key plotters. No, not *that* Throckmorton. Not the Protestant Sir Nigel Throckmorton who'd been Queen Elizabeth I's ambassador when Mary was in the French court. *This* Throckmorton was the Catholic Sir Francis Throckmorton. *This* Throckmorton was part of yet another plan for Catholic Spain to invade England, and for Mary to be freed and made queen. (And it's more than likely that Mary herself knew the outline of these plans at the very least.) *This* Throckmorton ended up being arrested in 1583, horribly tortured and then executed. The main problem with this plot was that the Charles Padget at the centre of it was – unknown to Throckmorton and the other plotters – a spy working for Sir Francis Walsingham, head of the English secret service.

THE PARRY PLOT

Next, the Parry plot was exposed. It turned out that a Dr Parry – who'd once had a shady job with Queen Elizabeth's government – planned to assassinate the English queen. Worse for Mary, Parry appeared to be working with a man called Thomas Morgan, Mary's own envoy in France! The last thing Mary wanted was for people to think she was involved in another plot to harm her cousin . . . She didn't want to lose what little goodwill Elizabeth might have left.

FEELING LOW

Mary was now at her lowest and things were about to get worse. After being in the kind care of Shrewsbury and Bess of Hardwicke, she was then put under the charge of firm-but-fair Sir Ralph Sadler. When January 1585 came around, however, Mary was not only handed over to the not-so-nice Sir Amyas Paulet but she was also moved back to Tutbury Castle, which she loathed and hated.

A TRUE PRISON

This time round, Mary's imprisonment was to be tougher than ever before. She wouldn't even be allowed in the castle grounds or courtyards to take walks, let alone go for rides. Paulet also did all he could to stop Mary sending or receiving letters, which, in the past, had been smuggled to and from her castle prisons by her servants. Mary complained that he acted as though she was a common criminal, not a crowned queen.

THE BABINGTON PLOT

Later in the year, after complaints at her treatment by the French, Mary moved to Chartley Hall, owned by the Earl of Essex. She was ill during the move, and ill for some time after. It was whilst she was there that the Babington plot, which was to lead to her downfall, unfolded. What's not clear is whether Walsingham's secret agents started the whole plot in the first place (to discredit Mary) or whether they became involved later, once the plotting was underway. What *is* clear is that, in 1586, a wealthy Catholic called Sir Anthony Babington led a plot to overthrow Queen Elizabeth with – surprise, surprise – the King of Spain . . . at least he hoped the king would be involved. From what we've seen already, that was probably a bit unlikely!

OVER A BARREL

Babington found a way of getting coded messages to and from Mary. On 16 January 1586, she was handed a message by Gilbert Gifford, who explained that it had been smuggled in using a leather pouch hidden inside a barrel of beer . . . and that she could send out secret messages in the same way. Sure enough, the messages were put in leather pouches inside barrels and smuggled in and out. What poor old Mary and the genuine plotters didn't know was that these messages were then read by Gifford and even Mary's jailer, Paulet, before being passed on. The

Protestant English knew exactly what Mary and Babington were up to.

YOU'RE NICKED!

The genuine plotters were arrested in August and Babington was taken to the Tower of London. He was soon made to confess because, thanks to Walsingham's men, his interrogators already knew all the facts anyway. He named Mary Queen of Scots as one of the conspirators.

TRICKED!

Inside her prison at Chartley, Mary herself had no idea what was going on in the outside world. When Paulet suggested they go for a ride on 11 August, she was pleased. When horsemen galloped towards them, she assumed they might be Babington plotters sent to free her. They were, in fact, the Queen of England's men there to arrest her. After a couple of weeks as a prisoner in a house at Tixall, Mary returned to Chartley, where her rooms had been thoroughly searched and many of her belongings taken. The next stop was Fotheringhay Castle in Northamptonshire which, by a twist of fate, had once belonged to a king of Scotland!

A TRIAL OF SORTS

Mary's trial began at Fotheringhay Castle on 15 October. She wore black and, riddled with rheumatism, had to be helped to her chair. She had hoped to be helped to the *throne* and was surprised and angry. Elizabeth did not attend. When Mary had a chance to speak, she accused Walsingham of creating the plot out of thin air, and Elizabeth's right-hand man, Cecil, of executing Catholics for being Catholics and nothing more. On the second day of the trial, she pointed out that not even the cleverest man in the room would have a chance of defending himself at such a trial, so what chance did she have? Everything was stacked against her.

A VERDICT IS REACHED

After the trial, and away from Fotheringhay Castle, the trial commissioners met in the Star Chamber in London. They declared Mary Queen of Scots guilty. The death sentence was passed. At the end of November, Mary spent two days writing a batch of farewell letters, which she passed on to her servants. In a number she argued that, if Elizabeth died childless, the Catholic king of Spain should get the English crown, not her own son James, unless he became a Catholic. The letters weren't delivered for many months because the poor servants themselves were imprisoned!

THE PLEAS TO SAVE HER

The protests of Mary's son, King James VI of Scotland, that his mother's life be spared were somewhat half-hearted. He was more interested in keeping in the Queen of England's good books so that he wouldn't ruin the chances of inheriting the English crown from her. The French, however, were more committed to saving their former queen. As well as many official protests from the French ambassador in London, a special ambassador was sent over by the king to plead for Mary's life. But no luck. All that was left to be done was for cousin Elizabeth to sign the death warrant.

THE INK IS DRY

Once the warrant was signed, Elizabeth didn't pass it on to her ministers. She gave the impression that she was still reluctant to let her cousin Mary die, despite everything. This was a diplomatic move on her part. In the end, her

ministers decided to go ahead and arrange the execution anyway . . . which meant that, if things turned nasty with the Catholic countries as a result, Elizabeth could always claim that it was *her ministers* and not *she* who'd done the dirty deed.

THE FINAL DAYS

Even Mary's jailer, Paulet, seemed saddened when the time of the execution drew nearer. He wrote that he was sad to have lived to see that unhappy day. Walsingham arranged for Bull, the executioner, to be smuggled into the castle disguised as a servant, with the executioner's axe hidden in a trunk! Knowing she was to die soon, Mary asked for her chaplain to prepare her soul for entering heaven. This was denied. Asking when she was to die, she was told, 'Tomorrow at eight o'clock'.

THE NIGHT BEFORE . . .

That night, Mary divided her belongings up into piles, each to be left to different people, ranging from loyal servants to Catherine de' Medici. She arranged everything down to the last detail. This done, she lay on her bed surrounded by her loyal ladies-in-waiting, each already dressed in black, ready for what was to come. She had been Elizabeth's prisoner for over eighteen years.

. . . THE DAY OF EXECUTION

The day of 8 February 1587 dawned. After saying goodbye to her attendants, and brief prayers, 44-year-old Mary was led into a room with 300 spectators. She wore a black dress with a white veil, clutched a prayer book and a crucifix and held her head high. Refusing to join in a Protestant prayer – saying that she was a Catholic and would 'spend [her] blood in defence of it' – she prayed out loud for her son James VI and for Queen Elizabeth. Then, following tradition, she forgave Bull, the executioner, and his assistants. Then they undressed her down to her dark red petticoat. It was also tradition that the executioner keep any of the ornaments she'd been wearing, but she asked that the rosaries tucked in her belt be given to particular friends. The executioner would be given money instead. Although many of her female attendants were in flood of tears by now, Mary seemed almost calm.

THE FINAL BLOW

With a white cloth wrapped around her head, a bit like a turban, Mary Queen of Scots knelt on a cushion and laid her neck on the block. Bull's first blow chopped the back of her *head* instead of her neck. (Some people claimed they heard Mary whisper 'Sweet Jesus'.) The second blow almost cut right through her neck, but not quite. The axe had to be used a third time but, even then, the story is not over.

AN EXTRAORDINARY END

Bull lifted Mary's severed head high by the hair, crying 'God Save the Queen' but – to his amazement and the crowd's horror – the head fell to the ground. What the executioner was left clutching was a brown wig! Mary's head on the floor had short, grey hair . . . and her lips were still moving, some say in silent prayer, for about a quarter of an hour. If that wasn't bad enough, Mary's pet dog, Skye, now appeared from under Mary's petticoat where it'd been hiding, and refused to leave its lifeless mistress.

LAID TO REST

So, with Mary Queen of Scots well-and-truly dead, this book is at an end. Queen Elizabeth pretended to be outraged that the execution had been carried out without her say-so, but few were convinced by this act. She did, indeed, die childless and Mary's son James, as well as being King James VI of Scotland, became King James I of England in 1603. Mary was originally buried in Peterborough but James had her body brought to Westminster Abbey in great splendour. She had wanted to be buried in France, but Elizabeth had forbidden this.

AN AFTERTHOUGHT

There's one weird fact that may not have occurred to you but, if you go back through the book, you'll see it's true. Despite the fact that each played such an important part in the other's life and, in the case of Mary, her eventual death, Queen Elizabeth I of England and Mary Queen of Scots never actually met each other face-to-face. Not even once. Ever.

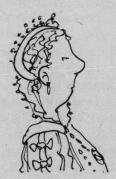

TIMELINE
At home and abroad

1542	Mary is born in December. Mary becomes Queen of Scots when her father dies in December.
1543	King Henry VIII of England arranges engagement between Mary and his son Edward. Mary crowned at Stirling Castle.
1547	English defeat Scots at Pinkie Cleugh.
1548	Mary leaves Scotland for France.
1558	Mary marries the dauphin, Francis. Elizabeth becomes Queen of England.
1558	*England loses Calais to France.*
1559	Mary becomes Queen of France too.
1560	Mary's mother dies. So does Mary's husband, now King Francis II of France.
1561	Mary returns to Scotland. *Sir Francis Bacon is born. Some people think he actually wrote Shakespeare's plays.*
1564	*William Shakespeare himself is born. (I wonder what HE thought?)*
1565	Mary marries Lord Darnley.
1566	Riccio is murdered. Mary gives birth to son James.
1567	Lord Darnley is murdered. Mary marries Bothwell, surrenders to the Protestants and is taken to Lochleven. Son James is made King James VI of Scotland.
1568	Mary escapes from Lochleven and flees to England, becoming a virtual prisoner for the rest of her life.
1586	Mary is arrested and tried for her part in the Babington Plot.
1587	Mary is executed.